Life is Always VI

Assisted Dying or Living?

Martin Ifeanyi Onuoha

ISBN: 9798396822245

Published with Barnes & Noble Press

DEDICATION

I wish to dedicate this book to my family, friends, and all who, in one way or another, have assisted me in answering God's call, as I mark my 50th birthday and the 22nd anniversary of my priestly ordination.

In a special way, I dedicate it to my late mother, Nneoha Celestina Onuoha, who, supported by her family and several medical professionals, endured the pain of cancer till life's natural end, and to my father, Nze Donatus Onuoha, who is gradually approaching his nineties and remains grateful for the gift of longevity, and for the love and support of family, friends, and his local community.

I would also like to dedicate it to my great friend and big brother, Msgr. Ray Walden, as he retires this year after decades of fruitful ministry with exemplary devotion and pastoral zeal.

CONTENTS

ACKNOWLEDGMENTS

I am grateful to God for the successful completion of this project. This is the fruit of a request by the Dean at our Clergy Deanery Conference to provide some literature to equip the clergy and lay people in our deanery for an enlightened engagement in the raging arguments for and against the Assisted Dying Bill. I am therefore grateful to the Dean and all the clergy of the deanery for throwing such a challenge to me, enabling the realisation of this project. I also appreciate the generous words of endorsement by the Council of Priests in the Diocese of Shrewsbury, recommending the original text to all priests in the diocese.

I am most humbled that the Archbishop of Westminster and President of the Bishops' Conference of England and Wales, His eminence, Cardinal Vincent Nichols, found the time to read through these pages and even availed me of the services on his expert in the field. Their comments, highlighting some repetitions in the text and that the Hippocratic oath is no longer taken at doctors' graduation here in the United Kingdom, elicited a few changes in this edition.

I am indebted to Bishop Mark Davies for his fatherly support and for graciously writing the foreword to this book. My gratitude extends to Bernard Beatty for his invaluable help in proofreading and editing this work, to Max Eden for the cover design, and to all those who allowed their stories to be anonymously shared in these pages to drive home our message.

My deep appreciation also goes to Diane and the entire Kurtz family, Joe and Brenda Dugan, John Kennedy, Joannie and Jim Bell, Linda and Richy Maurer, Diane and Rich Smith, Mark and Barbara Spencer, Albert and Kathy Quiroz, David and Cristina Golding, and Alan and Susan Johnston, for their friendship and support.

Last but certainly not least, I thank all my parishioners, past and present, for their love and helpful collaboration.

Life is Always Worth Living: Assisted Dying or Living?

FOREWORD

Father Martin Onuoha is well-known as a dedicated pastor and teacher of theology, with two published volumes on the Blessed Virgin Mary. The debate in the United Kingdom about so-called "Assisted Dying" has prompted these reflections drawn from his theological learning and his extensive pastoral experience. The reflections in their original form were warmly welcomed by parishioners and clergy and are now gathered into this one volume "Life is Always Worth Living".

Father Martin makes a significant and accessible contribution to the euthanasia debate in these pages. The late Cardinal Francis George once observed that people today are uneasy with arguments from principles. This sadly results in public discussion being limited to comparing examples with whoever can find the worst-case scenario winning the day. Yet, laws based on this kind of reasoning are not well-founded. Cardinal George insisted the truth is the truth, and we always need to find ways to be witnesses to the truth kindly and persistently. This is what Father Martin has set out to do, by offering the unchanging principles of Christian morality and seeking to illustrate them with examples from his own experience.

Father Martin sees it as no coincidence that a recent parliamentary debate sought to open the doors to euthanasia on the Feast Day of Pope Saint John Paul II. This great Saint and Pope of our time, who gave courageous witness to the Gospel of Life and the spiritual struggle with the 'culture of death,' is found throughout these pages as a guide and companion.

I wish to thank Father Martin Onuoha for his witness to the sanctity of human life and entrust the fruitfulness of this witness to the prayers of Pope Saint John Paul II.

+ Mark

Bishop of Shrewsbury

31st May 2023, Feast of the Visitation of the Blessed Virgin Mary.

'In this timely book, Fr. Martin Onuoha examines the arguments in favour of euthanasia and physician-assisted suicide and exposes their connection to distorted notions of eugenics, dualism, and autonomy. Drawing upon the African recognition of the sacredness of human life and the wisdom of Pope St. John Paul II, Fr. Onuoha argues that those who want to die are really in need of a personal affirmation of their dignity. Fr. Onuoha enriches his theological and moral analysis with personal stories of those who rediscovered their worth once their dignity was affirmed by others.'

Robert L. Fastiggi, Ph.D.

Bishop Kevin M. Britt Chair of Dogmatic Theology and Christology, Sacred Heart Major Seminary, Detroit, Michigan USA

'With clarity and power, Martin Onuoha explains why euthanasia cuts at the very heart of human society. Indeed, the praise that this book merits is simple: namely, this book must be read. Are some people's lives no longer of any value? Is opposition to euthanasia merely a hardhearted insistence that

others must suffer to the bitter end, in the name of abstract principle? In response, Martin Onuoha brilliantly challenges us to enact real and true compassion.'

Professor Matthew Levering,
James N. Jr. and Mary D. Perry Chair of Theology, Mundelein Seminary, USA.

'We need to think clearly about euthanasia. Is it good or bad? Should it be illegal or not? Assisted Living or Assisted Dying addresses these questions directly and openly. It does so in four different ways. Martin Onuoha examines the argument in favour and shows that they do not stand up to scrutiny. He does not deny the intensity of feelings aroused by euthanasia but warns against sentiment clouding judgement. Secondly, the book sets out the huge impact of legalising euthanasia which changes the character of medicine and hospital care, puts undue pressure on the infirm and elderly, and alters the understanding of human life. Here the book uses the careful and authoritative teaching of St John Paul II on the sanctity and given character of life. Finally, Martin Onuoha draws on

his experience of those who are set on ending their lives and how they can be helped to change their mind.'

Bernard Beatty

PREFACE

In 1920, when two German professors, Karl Binding and Alfred Hoche, conceived the idea of 'Life unworthy of life '(in their *Allowing the Destruction of Life Unworthy of Life*), no one would have imagined the impending annihilation that lurked. The phrase and idea subsequently became foundational to the Nazi designation of some fragments of the society – mainly people with epilepsy, alcoholism, birth defects, hearing loss, mental illnesses, personality disorders, vision loss, developmental delays and even those who suffered from certain orthopedic problems[1] - as not worthy of life, leading to mass exterminations. From the granting of a petition to kill one severely disabled child, this spiralled into what became known as mercy killing or euthanasia. It soon became a tool for advancing racial supremacy/purification, and for making hospital beds and personnel available for the looming war.[2] This was so surreptitiously and strategically executed that in the words of Hitler's own chief medical officer, the view was that this would be implemented 'more smoothly and rapidly in time of war' since, 'in the general upheaval of war, the open resistance anticipated from the church would not play the part it might in other circumstances'.[3] Thus, 'life unworthy of life' theory was progressively implemented first through coercive sterilization, the killing of "impaired" children in hospitals, the killing of "impaired" adults, and then it was eventually extended unimpeded to '"impaired" inmates of concentration and extermination camps and, finally, to mass killings, mostly of Jews'.[4] As the saying goes, 'those who do not learn history are doomed to repeat it'.[5]

In the face of the current UK parliamentary debate on the Assisted Dying Bill, I had been asked by the Dean to help by providing a guide for our extremely busy clergy in the deanery for the education of parishioners on this matter. When it dawned on me on the morning of the debate that it was actually holding on the feast day of St. John Paul II who, through his teaching and witness, was a stalwart advocate of the respect for human life from conception to its natural end, I got the impetus that I needed to execute this urgent task. It became obvious to me how the words of John Paul II[6] have as much, probably more, resonance for our time than his own. The unexpected, very positive reception of my article, which was later published by The Catholic Universe and recommended by the Council of Priests for priests in the diocese, has alerted me to the need for more work on this issue. Observing how easy it has been to change people's strongly held opinions on this matter simply by presenting the counterarguments to the mainstream propaganda, and how much they lament the dearth of such voices in the public space, have challenged me, on my 50th birthday, to publish this little book as a tiny drop in the ocean. It is my hope that it is a significant drop all the same.

I would like to begin with a reasoned caveat on the perils of a legal authorisation of euthanasia. It may seem odd to do so even before defining the concept itself, but I hope this break with conventional structure serves the intended purpose of attracting attention to real dangers in the present situation. An appraisal of the arguments in favour of euthanasia will be followed by wider considerations on the nature of human life. Some strong personal experiences, recounted in real-life stories, will set the tone for our conclusion which supports Saint John Paul II's opposition to the legalisation of euthanasia (see appendix) and counsels that efforts and resources ought to be channelled towards Assisted Living and not Dying.

CHAPTER ONE

Dangers of Legalising Euthanasia

What are the dangers of legalising euthanasia? Most of those in favour of euthanasia would want it to be legalised but the two things are not quite the same. Legislation for specific purposes often has unintended consequences quite different from those originally intended. The mainspring of most support for it is in understandable sentiment—the avoidance of suffering and the primacy of individual choice—but neither morality nor legislation can be based simply on sentiment. Any action proceeds from assumptions and produces effects. The assumption that euthanasia would be at the free request of an individual and that the consequence would be simply the avoidance of suffering is not at all likely to be the only, or indeed the main, consequence of its legalisation.

David Steel, for instance, who was the principal instigator for the legalisation of abortion, and still stands by that, has said that he is appalled by the present extent of abortions which often are used as a form of contraception. He did not intend this, but it happened, and it could have been foreseen. It is virtually certain that, after a while, the legalisation of euthanasia would turn it from an event in abnormal circumstances (the termination of suffering which cannot be substantially alleviated) into something much more normative for old people. It would become expected and, if not actually enforced, then encouraged. And the effect would not simply be on the elderly. Here, the manner of thinking that underlied Binding and Hoche's Allowing the Destruction of Life Unworthy of Life a century ago with such disastrous consequences would again authorise inhuman actions. Their phrase 'unworthy of life' is the inversion of our phrase 'quality of life'. Once we substitute 'quality of life' for 'human life' as primary value then those human lives without this 'quality' (usually determined in the crudest of ways) become 'unworthy of life'. This extends far beyond the elderly.

The Dutch government, for instance, has recently legalised euthanasia for those under twelve. Who decides on this quality of life and, more importantly, if it became customary, who would come to make the decisions in the future and on what grounds? Would those grounds shift in time? It is more than likely, for example, that the criteria would not simply be on the impairment of individuals but the effects of that impairment on families and resultant financial costs to the State. The latter is not a fanciful possibility. Chelsea Clinton, for instance, said that "American women entering the labour force from 1973 to 2009 added $3.5 trillion to our economy. The net, new entrance of women -- that is not disconnected from the fact that Roe became the law of the land in January of 1973." What is valued here is the apparent economic gains from the legalisation of abortion. Would anyone in 1973 have dared to use this argument? Not at all. It would have been regarded with horror. The argument at that stage was based mainly on sentiment—the picture of back street abortions with all the resultant dangers being replaced by routine hospital appointments which could be represented through euphemisms - 'termination of pregnancy', 'reproductive rights', or 'reproductive health' which avoid mentioning the destruction of a child. The picture in the mind is of a relieved woman. But 50 years later it is possible to hail economic gain and a larger labour force as a significant justification without any such picture in the mind. If euthanasia were legalised now, on the bases of singular cases and sentiment, would this still be the case in 50 years' time? Of course not. We would be in a different and frightening world where it would not pay to be anything but young and healthy with the resultant pressure for everyone to try as hard as possible to appear so.

What would be the nature of this pressure? Its most powerful and insidious character would be in a conformity to expectations. The 1920s Germany of Binding and Hoche was reeling from the effects of World War I but, in comparison with most countries, both men and women were well educated, and it had complex philosophical and musical traditions, yet it was this society which a decade later put up no substantial opposition to a regime that began to exterminate those whom it considered unfit. Respect for human life as such was replaced by value only recognised in healthy Aryan life. This was not done out of any sympathy with human suffering, rather the reverse, but it cut adrift from the moral understanding of most human cultures by redefining life than respecting it as a given. Why did the bulk of the German population go along with this? Doubtless fear and repression played their part and relief at the alleviation of unemployment and inflation associated with the new regime, but people increasingly conformed to what was expected of them. Their horizons shifted and narrowed. The Nuremberg Laws of 1935 officially made Jews second-class citizens and this and subsequent legislation undoubtedly influenced German opinion and behaviour for the worse, the effects of which are still rued to date.

The effect of legislation which allows something that once was not allowed is not simply to authorise this but give authority to the assumptions that underly the change. These assumptions, in turn, now exert pressure on everyone including those who do not share them. Those who continue to believe that there is intrinsic and peculiar value to human life as such can be presented as out of date or even callous. Many doctors, statistics seem to suggest that they are in the majority, are opposed to legalising euthanasia not so much on ethical grounds but because it alters the whole nature of their profession and their relation to patients. Here for example is the joint statement adopted by the 70th World Medical Association General Assembly, Tbilisi, Georgia, in October 2019. It declares: 'The WMA reiterates its strong commitment to the principles of medical ethics and that utmost respect has to be maintained for human life. Therefore, the WMA is firmly opposed to euthanasia and physician-assisted suicide.... No physician should be forced to participate in euthanasia or assisted suicide, nor should any physician be obliged to make referral decisions to this end. Separately, the physician who respects the basic right of the patient to decline medical treatment does not act unethically in forgoing or withholding unwanted care, even if respecting such a wish results in the death of the patient.'[7]

The present Hippocratic Oath foregrounds 'caring for the sick, promoting good health and alleviating pain and suffering.' Euthanasia, like suicide, is ending pain and suffering not alleviating it and manifestly it is not 'promoting good health'. The foundational ethics of medical practice would have to be overturned if this happened. The human consequences of such a change are unavoidable. Doctors would be divided amongst themselves. What began as a voluntary possibility of opting out would soon become inadmissible. As a result, inviting a doctor into your house or going to hospital would, in many cases, now become subject to second thoughts since it might involve a risk-laden exposure to pressure to agree to a termination or have this authorised by a 'caring' but sometimes calculating relative. Professor William L. Toffler, MD., narrates a concerning scenario in the state of Oregon: 'The change in attitude within the healthcare system itself is also deeply troubling. People with serious illnesses are now sometimes fearful of the motives of doctors and consultants. A few years ago, "Katherine," a patient with bladder cancer, contacted me. She was concerned that her oncologist might be one of the "death doctors". Katherine questioned his motives, particularly after consulting a second oncologist who was more sanguine about her prognosis and treatment options. Whether or not one or the other consultant was correct, such fears were never an issue before assisted suicide was legalized.'[8]

These arguments are not scare tactics. Any responsible action has to envisage the possible and, even more, the probable resultant effects. Would the legalisation of euthanasia result in a world substantially the same as the present but with the advantage of removing extreme suffering in a comparatively small number of difficult cases or would it result in a very different world where the nature and powers of medical practice have substantially altered, and government-enforced policies based on ethics which only recognises values in the 'quality of life' would now have all manner of unpleasant consequences? You do not need to be a doctor to recognise where human life is present and where it is not. It is a universal recognition. But there is no universal recognition of what 'quality of life' means. Here is a healthy woman of twenty walking down a street and here is Helen Keller who lost sight and hearing when she was 19 months old. If she had been born in the Netherlands today would she, at that age, still be allowed to live because of sentiment—'what a dreadfully limited life, what a strain on the parents and carers'— or would she be allowed (who would do the allowing and in what name?) to live until 88 as she did after gaining a degree, writing books, doing all manner of good works, and considered by Time magazine as amongst the most important hundred people in the Twentieth Century? But, on most 'quality of life' criteria, she would be a prime candidate for euthanasia where the healthy twenty-year-old woman would not. Helen Keller is an extreme case of course but who could tell that at 19 months old? Evidently, some 'experts' in the Netherlands can.

If euthanasia were to become legal in the United Kingdom, then the whole basis of law would have shifted. This is already the case to some extent because of legalising abortion, but the effects of legalising euthanasia would be much more pervasive and dramatic. Law would, in effect if not in intention, now privilege the interests of the healthy over the less healthy (the former has more intrinsic value than the latter) and would have trumped and displaced all extra political authorising (religious, ethical, inherited) as to the nature, and implicitly the purpose, of human life. That was also the case in both Nazi and Communist regimes but, historically, it has not been the case here in the United Kingdom.

Rather we should accept that we receive life rather than confidently defining its character in absurdly simple terms. The Hippocratic Oath should widen its scope since we now have much greater ability to alleviate suffering than earlier ages and the Hospice Movement, something of which we in our time can be proud, has had hugely beneficial effects in end-of-life care. Legalising euthanasia would reverse these gains. Why research means to help people in considerable pain or bother about finding experienced and sympathetic carers for them if the problem can be solved, both quickly and cheaply, by inviting them— in time encouraging them or, worse still, compelling them — to have an injection which ends it? Professor William L. Toffler describes the ordeal of Barbara, a retired school bus driver who, sadly, learned this lesson first-hand. Battling cancer, her oncologist had prescribed a drug that could increase the chance of her being alive in one year by 45%. The State denied the treatment as expensive for such a prognosis. 'Yet in the same letter denying coverage for her medication, the State offered full coverage (100%) for her assisted suicide.'[9]

There are other, probably incidental, arguments — the legalisation would make it very difficult to determine whether the elderly man who helps his wife, suffering intense pain, to die actually killed his wife against her wishes. This would require something like a written declaration by whoever is consenting to be killed by another which would be bureaucratic and capable of forgery. The list can go on.

Sentiment which provokes this state of affairs will not be able to determine its character. It is a very slippery slope, and we should not abandon the steady ground of reason and faith by letting understandable but misguided sympathy for those who suffer, together with our own fear of suffering, push us down it.

CHAPTER TWO

Appraising the Arguments for Euthanasia

Derived from two Greek words, eu (good or well) and thanasia (death), the word originally meant "a good or happy death"[10]. But over time the term euthanasia has come to designate one of the indices of "the culture of death" called mercy killing, which has been described as "an action or an omission which of itself or by intention causes death, in order that all suffering may in this way be eliminated"[11]. It is distinguished from suicide mainly by the fact that it is not the killing of self by self, but by another[12] person even if with consent or on request. It is also differentiated from assisted suicide which is "the act of making a means of suicide available to a patient",[13] by the fact that the patient himself is the principal cause of the termination of life while the physician formally cooperates as an instrumental cause of the action.

What are the arguments presented in its favour? In the previous chapter, I singled out the avoidance of suffering and the principle of individual autonomy. The former proceeds from natural sympathy but the latter depends upon assumptions that are often presumed to be rational, even self-evident. So, I want to unearth and face these assumptions. It appears quite plausible to suggest that "the most important aspect of having a right to life is that one can choose whether or not to invoke it."[14] For the proponents of euthanasia, "death control like birth control is a matter of human dignity. Without it persons become puppets"[15]. The customary arguments are these:

- If life is a gift, then the beneficiary may do with it as he pleases.

- We are not obliged to avail ourselves of the opportunity to perfect our souls that suffering presents.

- We may return a loan when we cannot care for it.

- Sentinels rendered incompetent should yield their posts.

- When it is impossible to use one's life for good, its termination is permissible.

- The special value of human life lies in its biographical dimension not in its biological one.[16]

Such arguments lead to the view that any sick person (though invariably the list widens beyond the sick) having requested aid to die, has a right to or ought to be aided. Thus, it is the duty of the physician, nurse, or relative to aid in dying.[17]

Manifestly, these arguments and, indeed, euthanasia in any form discard any notion that life is something received, and that human life has a sacred value in itself. Such concepts are not unique to Christianity. For example, it is a key precept of the Igbo value system, as expressed by the people of Nri: 'For the Nri, and the Igbo in general, human life is sacred, an absolute value. Any attempt on human life, even accidentally, must be purified'. Such attack on life ruptures the covenant between earth and heaven and calls for atonement.[18]

However, if these primary arguments on the basic character of human life do not persuade, then, there are a number of substantial empirical problems which would undoubtedly occur in any society that allowed (and bit by bit inevitably encouraged) euthanasia. These should give pause to any naive enthusiasm for 'assisted dying'. Human life is distinctively unique, with a world of difference between it and any other animal life. Hence, while animals in pain are 'put to sleep'(killed), historically this has not been the case with human beings (except sometimes wounded soldiers etc.). If the analogy holds and there is nothing special to human life, then all those with incurable diseases both mental and physical could in principle at the behest of state legislation be killed. On what grounds could it be resisted unless there is something inherently wrong in it? The Nazis may not have intended from the onset to kill Jews, but merely wanted to get rid of them from Germany—the sheer difficulty of doing this, the numbers involved, and the progressive attenuation of humanity and moral decency eventually precipitated the gruesome 'Final Solution'. But, from the beginning, as we have seen, Nazis did kill mentally defective people. A 1942 propaganda film (Dasein ohne Leben – Psychiatrie und Menschlichkeit [Existence Without Life – Psychiatry and Humanity]) openly advocated what had been Nazi practice even before the war. It distinguished Existence from Living and presented the mentally ill as merely existing and therefore with no right to life. Certainly, most people would be horrified by such homicide, but this is precisely the implicit distinction which is now used to justify 'assisted dying'. If no distinction is made between human and animal life in themselves and when some presumed norm or acceptable 'quality' of life is equated with life itself as opposed to mere existing, then it is impossible to produce good arguments against euthanasia and the likelihood of it being actually enacted in wholly secular societies (which only value quality of life) is high.

The problem is that once accepted it is impossible in thought (and therefore probably eventually in action) to prevent a whole series of frightening consequences. A practical example of such a consequence might sound preposterous but is not so if there is no intrinsically greater value in human life (because of its peculiar character) than in animal life. If your favourite dog was mauling a child, you might well not allow anyone to shoot the dog because it is of equal value to the child in itself, and you happen to love the dog more deeply. If the argument was that one should think of the suffering caused to the parents of the child, the reply could be that your feelings about the death of a favourite dog are just as important. To most people this suggestion and even my use of it as an argument feels ludicrous. And so, it is. But what arguments would there be to counter it in a world of relativism, consumerism, the elevation of individual choice, and the denial of any specifically sacred character to human life as such? Laws made with apparently good intentions and associated with positive values such as choice and compassion can have appalling consequences. There was no outcry in Germany when Dasein ohne Leben – Psychiatrie und Menschlichkeit was shown.

As noted by St. John Paul, the demand for euthanasia is often a hidden plea for more help[19] arising from what we could call 'social death.[20] The response should be to provide that caring concern of the medical staff and of the patient's family, which obviates the feelings of abandonment and worthlessness which so often lead to the desire for death.[21] Here is the evaluation of a medical expert, based on professional experience: 'Since assisted suicide became an option, I have had at least a dozen patients discuss this option with me in my practice. Most of the patients who have broached this issue weren't even terminally ill. One of my first encounters with this kind of request came from a patient with a progressive form of multiple sclerosis. "Joe" was in a wheelchair yet lived a very active life. In fact, he was a general contractor and quite productive. While I was seeing him, I asked him about how it affected his life. He acknowledged that multiple sclerosis was a major challenge and told me that if he got too much worse, he might want to "just end it." I responded, "It sounds like you are telling me this because you might ultimately want assistance with your own assisted suicide if things get worse." He nodded affirmatively, and appeared relieved that I seemed to understand. I told Joe that I could readily understand his fear and his frustration and even his belief that assisted suicide might be a good option for him. But, I added, should he become sicker or weaker, I would work to give him the best care and support available. I told him that no matter how debilitated he might become, at least to me, his life was and would always be inherently valuable. As such, I would not recommend, nor could I participate in, his assisted suicide. Joe simply said, "Thank you."

The truth is that we are not isolated, self-sufficient individuals. Every human being is part of a huge network of interdependent relationships with others. How physicians respond to the patient's request for lethal drugs can have a profound effect on a patient's choices as well as on his view of himself and his inherent worth. When a patient says I want to die, it may simply mean I feel useless. When a patient says I don't want to be a burden, it may really be a question, Am I a burden? When a patient says I've lived a long life already, she may really be saying I'm tired. I'm afraid I can't keep going. And finally, when a patient says I might as well be dead, he may really be saying No one cares about me. Many studies show that assisted suicide requests are almost always for such psychological or social reasons.'[22]

The advocates of voluntary euthanasia need also to be reminded of the very thin borderline between voluntary, involuntary, and non-voluntary euthanasia. The decision will almost inevitably be taken either at a time of great distress or so far in advance (through an advance directive or living will) that the decision is hypothetical; the patient may be suffering from clinical depression; the influence of relatives and doctor may be weighty, though subtle.[23] I will cite very moving instances of this latter.

Another problem which will certainly arise where the law is changed in favour of Assisted Dying/Euthanasia is a new and deadly form of paternalism which indeed represents an inversion of patient autonomy. For instance, consider that Mr A has made a reasonable or justified request for euthanasia, what is the standing of Mr B, whose circumstances are the same, yet who has not made such a request? Surely Mr B is then unreasonable and unjustified in deciding to continue using costly resources and placing considerable strains on relatives and on the medical and nursing staff and, in some cases, on the taxpayer.[24] I refer here to one of the interventions of Danny Kruger, the MP for Devizes, to the parliamentary debate: 'The main argument for assisted dying is the simple one of autonomy. I think a lot of the support for assisted dying comes from the simple and natural resentment that anybody should try to stop people doing what they want, especially about something as important as this—literally a matter of life and death. But in this case, things are the other way around for many people. In my view, we need to keep assisted dying illegal because, as a matter of practical fact, for many people, it would narrow their autonomy. It would reduce their freedom substantially, because it would put them on a path with only one destination. That is because of the incentives that assisted dying would introduce. The first incentive would be in our healthcare system. The simple, blunt fact is that it is cheaper for the system to help people end their life early than to care for them for weeks, months or years. That is not an argument we hear for assisted dying, but it is compelling. The cat was let out of the bag rather when the Member of the Scottish Parliament who is trying to legalise assisted dying in Scotland cited research from Canada showing that the health service there has saved hundreds of millions of dollars in care costs. We see, in contradiction to a point made by the Hon. Member for Gower, that where assisted dying is introduced, investment in palliative care stalls or recedes in comparison with countries where assisted dying is illegal. Meanwhile, in Oregon, we see people being refused palliative care on cost grounds and then choosing assisted dying because there is no other option. I know we pretend that we do not have rationing in the NHS, but obviously, with finite resources, we do. Do we really imagine that assisted dying will not become an option that doctors and medical managers will not tacitly—even unintentionally—encourage?'[25]

What seems unlikely now can become an accepted commonplace. Euthanasia, though often justified (as abortion has been) through difficult cases which involve suffering from which we naturally recoil, is primarily a simplified rationalism which can only find value in the exercise of health, intelligence, the pleasurable, and social comforts. It depends upon exactly the same crude rationalised eugenics adopted in Germany in the darkest period of its history.

Euthanasia presents itself as bright (as eugenics did then) but is always in league with darkness.

Voluntary euthanasia, then, is said to be justified by appealing to an absolute notion of human autonomy. But human autonomy, though real, is not absolute. It arises from the very dignity of man that is in question. Human autonomy cannot extend to that on which it is founded, and thus must be limited, as Pope John Paul II has always said.[26].

Active Involuntary Euthanasia ought to be ridiculously indefensible until one considers that the Nazi film distinguishing between existence and life is one that many found plausible, and that the Spartans killed unhealthy children as a matter of course and it is possible that some sort of euthanasia for the elderly and disabled was also practiced by them. In England, with the still current case of Dr. Harold Frederick Shipman who murdered hundreds of mostly sick and elderly patients, one wonders how anyone would advocate for the legalisation of such atrocity, giving a legal backing to such evident evil. However, as horrendous as it sounds, this will not be absurd if the only thing that one values is a strong healthy life. A slow but progressive deterioration into a Spartan mindset (though not through their glorification of war) seems to be increasingly on display. St. John Paul is unequivocal here: "The choice of euthanasia becomes more serious when it takes the form of a murder committed by others on a person who has in no way requested it and who has never consented to it. The height of arbitrariness and injustice is reached when certain people, such as physicians or legislators, arrogate to themselves the power to decide who ought to live and who ought to die".[27] He further warns that such morally bad choices as the arbitrary taking of innocent human life, not only poison society and dishonour the Creator, but "harm their perpetrators more than those who are harmed by them",[28] especially since it is an attack on the very human nature of which they are part.

Non-voluntary Euthanasia is often justified with the following arguments:

i. The 'Cartesian' dualistic distinction between "personal" life and biological life sees the body as an instrumental good for persons which should be set aside when it becomes a burden. In such a view, human beings are spirits encased in flesh.

ii. Non personhood claims that the subjects of euthanasia, although certainly members of the human species, are no longer to be regarded as persons because they lack presently exercisable cognitive faculties.

iii. The duty of the physician and agents of health care towards patients could be seen as arranging a peaceful death

And to these arguments will be added the familiar ones, which I have already set out, about quality of life and the natural impulse (presented even as a duty) to release from suffering those in severe pain and even in severe personal circumstances.

The wrong understanding of the composite nature of man inherent in the first argument is misleading. As St. Thomas taught, we are a composite; though the soul is the actuality of a living body, 'it is not the entire human being, and my soul is not I'.[29] The body is intrinsic to human persons, a constitutive part of their very reality.[30] Hence, the dualism often underlying euthanasia, as it does the alleged non-necessary connection between biology and gender (Pope Francis has called the propagation of such ideas to school children 'ideological colonisation') when the mind decrees otherwise, is false. The important point to note here is that, although the dignity of human life is most fully manifested in rational thinking, this is only a part of the activities which characterise the human person. "Therefore it is not only human beings actually capable of intellectual activity who are persons, but every living being, of a human body capable enough to be the bodily basis of some intellectual act".[31] Any talk of levels of intellection for the determination of humanness and the allotment of justice will be arbitrary.[32] Neither does humanness lie in the mere sequence of an individual's biographical life, since the givenness of our particular kind of being precedes and prescribes the kinds of actions of which we are capable.

These are real and important arguments of a deeper character than the customary interchange of opinions about euthanasia. But the 'quality of life' argument is much more pervasive since it is easy to understand, and it appeases our natural human desire for happiness and health. It precludes value but appears to support it. It is essential to oppose it openly for these reasons and to use arguments which can be widely understood.. St. John Paul, for example, points out that it makes man or a committee a judge over others as to who should or should not live. The criteria for such judgment cannot but be arbitrary although they will be dressed up in various rationalised jargons. For instance, various religious, cultural, and political persuasions and academic schools of thought have their own convictions on the value and telos of human life. On whose precepts will such judgment be based? Many spouses who visit their other halves who have dementia or Alzheimer's in hospitals and care homes on a daily basis do so not out of sheer duty or as a burden but in love, and cherish every moment with them, and so would not acquiesce to the quality-of-life argument. This argument intrinsically represents a dangerously simple application of Darwin's theory of the survival of the fittest[33], which if widely applied could also justify the elimination of the elderly or the wiping out of even some races that may be considered non-viable. In any event, the old phrase 'slippery slope' is exactly the right one.[34] Wherever euthanasia has been introduced (Holland, Belgium, some US states) it has always expanded beyond the original restrictions so that eventually the issue of free choice (apparently sacrosanct in the modern world!) becomes blurred — e.g., relatives giving permission for someone with dementia to be euthanised. The commonest reason given for elderly people requesting euthanasia where the law has been established for a while is not wanting to be a burden to relatives and carers. I can hardly express this better than Danny Kruger as he raises telling questions: 'Over half the people in countries where assisted dying is legal choose it because they feel they are a burden to their family. Tragically, a lot also say that they are lonely. Is that not terrible - people getting the state to help kill them because they do not want to be a burden on a family that never visits them? Talk to any hospice manager about relatives and they will quietly confirm it. There are a lot of people who want granny or grandpa to hurry up and die.'[35]

The basic command to love one's neighbour as oneself (a Christian ethic which is widely understood as the Golden Rule outside it) cannot be transformed into a judgement that a neighbour should die.[36] This is virtually self-evident. Hence, against the golden rule or mercy argument, Euthanasia must be called a false mercy, and indeed a disturbing "perversion" of mercy. True "compassion" leads to sharing another's pain and helping them to bear or alleviate it; it does not kill the person whose suffering we cannot ourselves bear. The act of euthanasia appears all the more perverse if it is carried out by those, like relatives, who are supposed to treat a family member with patience and love, or by those, such as doctors, who by virtue of their specific profession, are supposed to care for the sick person even in the most painful terminal stages.[37] The physician's duty ought to be at the service of life not its destruction.[38] The physician has an obligation to halt the natural course of the fatal illness only if he has a charge to help in some way and as long as he has this charge.[39] As I have already argued but it needs to be said over and over again, doctors and hospitals are bound to radically change character if euthanasia is introduced, and trust is eroded.

With Passive or Indirect Euthanasia, the case becomes most complicated, as we are faced with such questions as: i) Does it make a moral difference whether death is actively brought about rather than occurring because life-sustaining treatment is withheld or withdrawn? ii) Must all available life-sustaining means always be used, or are there certain extraordinary or disproportionate means that need not be employed? iii) Does it make a moral difference whether the patient's death is directly intended, or whether it comes about as a merely foreseen consequence of the agent's action or omission?[40]

It is fundamental here to distinguish between active killing and passive renunciation or "pulling the plug" of life-prolonging measures. In the first case the active cause of the patient's death is the intervention of the physician and not the sickness of the patient. This involves the inescapable culpability of the physician. In the second case the active cause of death is the illness. There is only the removal of medically and morally unwarranted artificial support that prolongs the dying process, allowing death to occur naturally.[41] The distinction is quite clear, and it is a moral one.

The distinction is made clearer in the answer to the second question. Discontinuing medical procedures that are burdensome, dangerous, extraordinary, or disproportionate to the expected outcome can be legitimate; it is the refusal of 'over-zealous' treatment. This is justified because here one does not will to cause death; one's inability to impede it is merely accepted.[42] Hence St. John Paul says, one can in conscience "refuse forms of treatment that would only secure a precarious and burdensome prolongation of life, so long as the normal care due to the sick person in similar cases is not interrupted"[43].

It is however necessary to specify the criteria for ascertaining that a means is ordinary or extraordinary, especially since even mistake in judgement is not considered excusable in this matter: "an act or omission which, of itself or by intention, causes death in order to eliminate suffering constitutes a murder …. The error of judgment into which one can fall in good faith does not change the nature of this murderous act, which must always be forbidden and excluded."[44]

Noting the need for this specification, the Declaration of 1981, to clear any possible ambiguity of the terms ordinary and extraordinary as used by Pope Pius XII[45], incorporated the terms proportionate and disproportionate. Yet specifying the latter remains a task. Even the exegesis of authors like K. O' Rourke, seeing the problem as solved by the Pope's phrase of "helping a person strive for the spiritual purpose of life"[46] is not conclusive. 'Extraordinary' here must mean 'disproportionate' but we have to tread carefully. For instance, some people who, for instance, have lost or never attained reasoning ability and in this sense cannot be said to strive for spiritual purpose in life (for example mentally impaired infants), might be considered unsuited to be treated for their wounds or illnesses since this is ineffective in pursuing the spiritual purpose of life in their case. But to think like this is to fall into the Cartesian trap of dualism where the body is a mere instrument of the soul rather than an intrinsic component of the human composite. A better interpretation should underline, among other things, the criteria of excessive burdensomeness and usefulness. Proportionate burdensomeness will consider factors like riskiness, side-effects, excessive pain, family, age etc. For instance, some treatments like amputation may be proportionate for a youth, but not for a cancerous old woman. John Dryden, the Seventeenth- Century poet, who converted to Catholicism, got gangrene in one leg - it was amputated (no anaesthetic) but then gangrene was found in the other leg. He refused to have that amputated and died of it. That is perfectly understandable but is not euthanasia for the intention was not suicidal in itself.

The elucidatory words of the Sacred Congregation for the Doctrine of the Faith are worth citing at length here: 'Everyone has the duty to care for his or he own health or to seek such care from others. Those whose task it is to care for the sick must do so conscientiously and administer the remedies that seem necessary or useful. However, is it necessary in all circumstances to have recourse to all possible remedies? In the past, moralists replied that one is never obliged to use "extraordinary" means. This reply, which as a principle still holds good, is perhaps less clear today, by reason of the imprecision of the term and the rapid progress made in the treatment of sickness. Thus some people prefer to speak of "proportionate" and "disproportionate" means. In any case, it will be possible to make a correct judgment as to the means by studying the type of treatment to be used, its degree of complexity or risk, its cost and the possibilities of using it, and comparing these elements with the result that can be expected, taking into account the state of the sick person and his or her physical and moral resources. In order to facilitate the application of these general principles, the following clarifications can be added: - If there are no other sufficient remedies, it is permitted, with the patient's consent, to have recourse to the means provided by the most advanced medical techniques, even if these means are still at the experimental stage and are not without a certain risk. By accepting them, the patient can even show generosity in the service of humanity. - It is also permitted, with the patient's consent, to interrupt these means, where the results fall short of expectations. But for such a decision to be made, account will have to be taken of the reasonable wishes of the patient and the patient's family, as also of the advice of the doctors who are specially competent in the matter. The latter may in particular judge that the investment in instruments and personnel is disproportionate to the results foreseen; they may also judge that the techniques applied impose on the patient strain or suffering out of proportion with the benefits which he or she may gain from such techniques. - It is also permissible to make do with the normal means that medicine can offer. Therefore one cannot impose on anyone the obligation to have recourse to a technique which is already in use but which carries a risk or is burdensome. Such a refusal is not the equivalent of suicide; on the contrary, it should be considered as an acceptance of the human condition, or a wish to avoid the application of a medical procedure disproportionate to the results that can be expected, or a desire not to impose excessive expense on the family or the community. - When inevitable death is imminent in spite of the means used, it is permitted in conscience to take the decision to refuse forms of

48

treatment that would only secure a precarious and burdensome prolongation of life, so long as the normal care due to the sick person in similar cases is not interrupted. In such circumstances the doctor has no reason to reproach himself with failing to help the person in danger.'[47]

The meaning of 'usefulness' in this context needs to be understood very precisely: 'in Catholic tradition a means has been judged useless in the strict sense if the benefits it promises are nil or useless, in a wider sense if the benefits conferred are insignificant in comparison to the burdens it poses.'[48] We must note that this is not a fall back to the errors of the "quality of life" argument, since what is at issue here is not the person but the means. Indeed, Catholic tradition "allowed quality of life considerations if they were related to the means themselves"[49] while repudiating them when applied to persons. This is a vital distinction. The whole argument against euthanasia depends upon ascertaining what is due to the 'human subject' as such and protecting this from unnoticed incursions into the territory of the 'human object'. If we are objects, we can be disposed of at will for this or that alleged reason but as human subjects with logos we cannot be treated as objects with a shelf life proportionate to the presence or absence of any 'quality'. It is appropriate in certain circumstances to distinguish the proportionate from the disproportionate, but we must avoid the all too easy methodology of "proportionalism" which would authorise apparent intended evil for an alleged proportionately greater good, since the evil of murder ('thou shalt not kill' has precisely this specific sense) must always be avoided. Yet euthanasia has the character of murder or self-murder despite its declared good intentions (and some murderers have, not implausibly, pleaded good intentions).

There needs, however, a clear distinction to be drawn between medication (which is relative to particular circumstances) and feeding (which is intrinsic to human life). In appropriate circumstances (where it can no longer avoid death or alleviate suffering) it is legitimate and good to withdraw medication. That is for the judgement of the doctor or nurse. But there are no appropriate circumstances in which feeding, if still possible, should be withdrawn and this exceeds the expertise and authority of the doctor or nurse. The distinction is especially necessary in the case of those said to be in PVS (Persistent or Permanent Vegetative State). On this I agree with J. Daniel Mindling's presentation of St. John Paul II's teaching. He comments: 'Especially in light of the tragic case of Terri Schiavo, Pope John Paul II left no doubt about the Church's clear teaching regarding those in a so-called "persistent vegetative state" (PVS). In the opinion of their doctors, these patients have suffered such severe neurological damage that they can no longer give any indication that they are aware of themselves or of their environment. It is unfortunate that their state is labeled "vegetative." Human persons are not vegetables. Such regrettable terminology may lead some to conclude falsely that these handicapped persons are more like vegetables than human beings. This is simply not true. All disabled persons have basic rights. Although their higher cognitive functions may be seriously impaired, these patients are human beings with the same intrinsic value and personal dignity as any other human person. Caution should be exercised even regarding the diagnosis of PVS. It is true that the longer such a state persists, the less likely the patient will recover. Nevertheless, at times this label is applied incorrectly, and there are more than a few cases reported in the literature of persons who have emerged from a "vegetative" state after appropriate treatment or who have recovered at least partially, even after many years. "We can thus state that medical science, up till now, is still unable to predict with certainty those, among patients in this condition, who will recover and who will not." PVS patients, like all other patients, have a right to basic health care. They should be kept comfortable, clean, and warm. Care should be taken to prevent complications associated with being confined to bed. They should be given appropriate rehabilitative care and monitored for signs of improvement. Families who bear the heavy burden of dealing with this condition should be assisted by the rest of society, as true solidarity demands.'[50]

Regarding the third question, on the direct intentionality of the act, a similarly precise and intelligible distinction must be applied in cases where there exists no direct causal link between induced unconsciousness and the shortening of life although the actual administration of drugs brings about two distinct effects, the one the relief of pain, the other the shortening of life. In such cases the action to administer such a drug is lawful.[51] Yet some necessary conditions need to be observed: Firstly, that there is, between these two effects, a reasonable proportion, and that the advantages of the one compensate for the disadvantages of the other;

Secondly, it is important also to ask oneself if the present state of science does not allow the same result to be obtained by other means; Thirdly, that in the use of the drug, one should not go beyond the limits which are actually necessary, as for instance to impede the fulfilment of moral and religious duties.[52] In all these cases, we need to think very carefully, maintain and refuse to surrender necessary distinctions all of which depend upon the sanctity (or at very least the special character) of human life whose origin and termination in this world can never be simply matters of utilitarian concern and overt control as though we were the authors of our existence and can do what we will with it.

CHAPTER THREE

Wider Considerations

All living human beings find themselves alive. They are born in a specific place and time to specific parents on whom they are dependent and awaken to a world around them. No one buys or earns their life, or from some imagined pre-existent place, has the option of choosing it. Tellingly, the Prefect of the Dicastery for the Doctrine of the Faith, Cardinal Ladaria Ferrer, sees a connection between our attempts to 'manufacture' life and the movement for euthanasia: 'First a sexuality without children was accepted, then the production of children without the sexual act. Life, once it is manufactured, is no longer considered a 'gift' per se, but a 'product' to which a value is attributed according to its utility. This utility, measured in concrete functions, is what is currently referred to as 'quality of life'. Quality of life is thus transformed into a discriminating concept between lives worthy and lives unworthy of being lived, which can therefore be suppressed: eugenic abortions, suppression of the disabled, euthanasia of the terminally ill, and so on. All this is mollified by a certain 'compassion' towards those in this situation (eliminating the sick), compassion towards their family members and towards a society that will rid itself of unnecessary costs.'[53] Such tendencies to 'produce' life underlie the trendy 'this is my life' culture which, ironically, promotes death.

Can it really be said, though, except in a loose sense, that we are given life since there is no 'we' in existence before our conception to whom life can be given? Unlike all other living beings, we alone know that we are going to die. That is why the Ancient Greeks called us 'mortals'. It was not because we are subject to death, for all observed life is so subject, but because we know that this is so. If life were strictly a gift, or we had somehow bought or acquired it, then it would be a possession that we could keep or throw away. But it is not.

This is why the expression 'this is my life' and the analogous one 'this is my body', with the corresponding assumption that we can do what we like with either, is mistaken. 'My' is grammatically a possessive adjective, and so it would seem that 'my' in these cases involves possession or ownership. But this is not the case. If, for example, I say 'this is my pen' then I will have come by the pen through gift or purchase. It is mine and I can do what I please with it including discarding it. But if I say that 'this is my hometown' or 'my country is a parliamentary democracy' then it is clear that 'my' here does not imply that I own my hometown or country. 'My', in this instance, is purely indicative. But there can be no question that the character and force of 'my' in 'my life' and 'my body' is similarly indicative rather than possessive for the 'I' comes into being at exactly the same moment as my body and my life. It does not exist in any domain where it can purchase or receive a body or life. This may seem a trivial point, but it is not.

We cannot choose whether to be born or find ourselves alive, but we do have subsequent choices. Our bodies will have certain given characteristics of health and form some of which we cannot alter but we can look after our bodies or neglect them, adjust our appearance etc. Similarly, we will encounter limits in our lives—not everyone can be a champion sprinter or a great artist—but we can make real choices as to careers, friends, where we live etc. We have much greater freedom than any other living creature that we know about. It is the absolute fundamentals of our existence that we cannot alter because they do not fall within what is 'mine'. Even an atheist must admit this. For a Christian, these fundamentals are the result of God's creation which is not simply a past act but intrinsic to present sustained life by his conservation or continued creation. If this is the case, then death — like conception and birth — does not fall within the same evident range of choices as to whether we take this or that path within our lives. It is bound up with the fundamentals of life which exceed our grasp and which we presuppose in everything that we do. We can talk of 'my birthday' but not of 'my birth' or 'my death' as though we own them and can simply determine their character. We are predefined by them. We can talk of 'my baby' or 'my child' but that does not imply ownership as though we could do what we like with them any more than 'my mother' or 'my father' does.

This is clear but it is not widely grasped partly because of the widespread, often aggressive, use of 'this is my body' or 'this is my life' as implying 'I can do what I please with them'. At the just concluded conference on Humanae Vitae, titled, 'My body belongs to me', Cardinal Ladaria Ferrer aptly exposes this as an erroneous 'anthropology that puts freedom before nature, as if they were two irreconcilable elements', a flawed exaltation of freedom, unrelated to truth, which presents 'desire and will as the ultimate guarantors of human decisions. That is why the phrase 'My body belongs to me' continues: 'and I will do with it what I want'. 'What I want' expresses desire alone as the guarantor of moral decision-making.' He recalls Paul VI's warning that 'before freedom there are certain meanings, which man can grasp thanks to reason, and which he did not choose, which regulate and direct his behaviour.'[54]

Heedlessness in this regard, under the unguarded tyranny of 'it is my body', ultimately leads to the reification and abuse of the body.

But there is a deeper reason too. Human beings dislike limits. Partly, this corresponds to something in us. The opening of St John's Gospel says that Logos was in the beginning with God and was God. Logos means both Hebraic Word and Greek Reason. That Logos is also in us. We are animals with Logos. That was the old Greek definition of human beings, and it became familiarised as 'rational animals'. We are uniquely made. 'Created in the image of God…human beings are beings who share the world with other bodily beings but who are distinguished by their intellect, love and freedom'.[55] So, there is something unlimited in us. In fact, the Church rightly sees herself as 'at once a sign and a safeguard of the transcendent character of the human person'.[56] But we are not God. We are bodily beings set in particular time and place and subject to death. Part of us revolts against our limitations and wants to be unlimited. The Adam and Eve story places this misdirection and hubris right at the beginning of human lives. It is repeated now in the demand to overthrow the limitations of being, like Adam and Eve, either male or female. No, it seems that we can randomly be whichever sex we choose to be and freely vacillate or occupy any blurred point between them. It is also evident in tendencies to transhumanism towards cyborgs. It is this kind of reasoning which makes euthanasia fit so easily into the loose parameters of modern thinking. Death is the ultimate human limit. If we can choose its manner and timing then we can diminish, even apparently control its sting. For a Christian, this has been wholly accomplished by Christ, the man-God. Since all things were made through Him, then it is possible for Him to do this. He enters wholly into Death and destroys its power. But this is beyond our anthropological limitations. We did not make all things and so any idea of absolute ownership is misguided and averse to our anthropological constitution.

There are two groups of people, roughly speaking, who are very strongly in favour of euthanasia. The first, understandably enough, is those who live with intolerable suffering and difficulty and wish above all else to have it ended together with some of their immediate family and friends. We cannot empathise enough with the agony of people in this group. The other, a much larger group which uses the first group as important reference, wishes to make euthanasia normal and legal because this would be a vital step towards establishing a new set of conditions which would govern human lives. These conditions would replace all inherited values, references, and customs and set up a world in which we are the authors of all moral norms and have unlimited freedom to do so. This would be in the name of freedom and progress but would be in effect a universal presumption to which all would have to bow to and accept. Disapproval, censorship, and legislation would back this up. Any religious or philosophical or common human acknowledgement of the other values ('the old values') would be discredited as unacceptable in a new and better world. Apparently, nothing is known of what precise principles this 'better' world would be founded on except its characteristic fluidity and erraticism. This is not of course the work of some coherent invisible group but the creed of the like-minded who seek to alter and displace common opinion so that the world is in accord with their opinions.

Two very different examples will illustrate the problem. The first is Body integrity dysphoria. This is a condition in which someone (usually male) has a strong interior conviction based upon the difference between their mental image of their body and their actual one that they ought to have a limb amputated or even become blind or deaf. This is a rare but real condition. Surgeons, when intreated to perform an amputation usually resist but there are cases (a Scottish surgeon called Dr Robert Smith for instance) where a medical expert has carried out these wishes. The argument must be that one should respect the desires and opinions of the person making the request. Most doctors, of course, are horrified by this since they are doing exactly the opposite of what doctors have always believed to be their calling—to cure sickness and alleviate physical suffering. But if individual opinion is primary and there are no other larger governing criteria then it is not easy to argue against it since the operation would, in principle at any rate, remove one kind of intense discomfort. The other example is quite different. In many universities, it is now common for some influential elements in the student body (and even some academics) to insist that any books or opinions that are out of step with theirs should be disallowed since this would cause them undue discomfort and not match their preferred view of the world. They are a small number, but they have had many successes. Books have disappeared from syllabuses, lecturers debarred from lecturing (in some cases losing their jobs) and visiting speakers prevented from speaking. The argument is based on strongly held opinions and the inadmissibility of any kind of intellectual discomfort. In both cases, the character of the argument and the assumptions are very close to those who strongly advocate euthanasia. It is obvious, except to these small influential groups, that if doctors should be able to practise amputation simply because someone wants it and if universities can only teach what some students already agree with, then the whole character of medicine and universities has completely altered. It is equally obvious that student insistence on the content and character of what they are taught cannot be based on anything profound because, self-confessed, they have never been exposed to any thoughts, opinions, or shades of feeling other than their own. What is common to these cases and the strong advocates of euthanasia is that their argument presupposes the absolute authority of private opinion (presented as progressive mantra) and the imposition of this on everyone else. The irony of it all is the sheer dictatorship, as these students do not want censorship only for themselves but for the entire student body and in a number of cases this has actually happened. The circumstances are entirely different, but the force of the 'argument' and the insidious effect of strident groups is exactly the same in all these cases. The difference is that most people are unsympathetic to these demands whereas in the case of euthanasia they can be strongly influenced by sentiment — natural sympathy for those in intolerable conditions. But the underlying argument and the results are, to all extents and purposes, not dissimilar. This is why, hard as it is, it is essential to accept, and sympathise, but always situate sentiment rather than let it be the overall governing factor. We are beings with Logos and must always try, so far as we can, to reason with the whole of our being and not trust to shifting sands.

Death is a condition of the life into which we are born with our mortal bodies. We have to accept it in the same way that we accept being human and alive. The truth of this is inescapable but it does not soften the difficulty of accepting, in our lives and that of others, intense suffering which can lead not only to the desire for death but occasion it. In such circumstances, we have to bear the force of opposed kinds of knowledge, impulses and desire within us as we often have to do, but this is an extreme case. If someone takes their own life or asks others to do so for them when pain and difficulties seem insurmountable, we can have sympathy and understanding for the person but not for the act. What is an apparently private matter and decision for them is in fact a universal declaration that we have authority over the fundamental conditions of our being which we can destroy even though we did not create it. If that is the case, then there is no Truth to which to attend, and human subjectivity is absolutised and cannot be guided by anything outside its own determinations. The effects of such anarchistic assumptions reverberate far beyond the issue of euthanasia and would return the world to the chaos and nothingness which God's creative act originally ordered into comeliness and form.

Generally, advocates of euthanasia have always been small in number but, at the present time, they are more numerous and often find ready ears that would not have listened in the past. Why is this? Many commentators have noted that, throughout the last decades, Western societies in particular have been strongly affected or, to put it more harshly, brain-washed by two quite opposed movements of thought which nevertheless clamp together in their operation. The first we could call liberal individualism. Here the individual is king and so free to make whatever choices they wish since there is said to be no larger context or authority or Truth apart from individual opinion – ditto the 'I' and 'My' mentality. This began as, roughly, a political philosophy rejecting inherited political and social conventions of all kinds but in recent years it has made an unholy alliance with consumer culture which, in principle, privileges individual choice but, in effect, gives power to the marketing strategies of large commercial concerns and interests. The consumer is more controlled than in control and either does not acknowledge this or has been conditioned to accept it.

In the same way—and this is the other dominant style of thought—we have become increasingly acceptant of all manner of restraints, often in association with newly declared 'values'—from which it is perilous to dissent and, increasingly, will be penalised for doing so. Any reader of this will be able to name examples. Thus, the alleged liberation movements from supposed outdated, autocratic, worldviews and systems become the new oppressors. These two movements which merge together 'this is my life' with 'life must be lived in this way and in these terms' have increasing confidence and power. The present demand for euthanasia is a perfect example of this double movement which produces a single result. The privileging of unlimited choice leads to conformity. The privileging of life under the banner of quality of life leads to death.

Modern history lessons often choose Nazi Germany and the Second World War for their subject. Communism — in the sense that it was believed in by many up until 1989 — is widely discredited. Both are associated, rightly, with unacceptable kinds of control. Both presented themselves as popular modern movements bringing a new and better world to the majority of people. Virtually no one thinks like this now and yet we are drifting into a world where the invocation of popular choice and new 'modern' values authorises a new order imposing far-reaching restrictions on what we are allowed to think and do. Euthanasia is a particularly telling example of this. It is presented as allowing individuals to end what they perceive as intolerable suffering or situation and thus defending the rights of the individual whilst reducing suffering in the world. Many commentators have noted that we have become a 'therapeutic society' in which the avoidance of suffering and discomfort has become the primary purpose of life, no other value is admitted. But the effects of introducing euthanasia as a recognised option, and legal availability, will not be to increase individual choice but rather to increase social control in areas where it has not historically been exercised and it will make the condition of all those who suffer more difficult since there is always an available, and even easy, end to it which carries social approval. Why then sympathise with or try to ameliorate suffering? We cannot predict the future but that something like this will happen if euthanasia is introduced is virtually certain. We must not sleepwalk into it.

But again, the question will be asked as to why we are now suddenly in danger of moving into a world as immoral and controlled, though claiming the opposite, as those of Nazi Germany and the Soviet Union. Both those, quite explicitly, rejected the Christian foundations of their societies and in doing so created an empty space in which compelling but extremely simplifying images of human life, human society, and human ends could be both advertised and enforced. We are in a not dissimilar situation. Those arguing in favour of euthanasia never take account of any principles other than individual choice and the avoidance of pain. It is as though they know what life, suffering, and death are and there can be no mysteries, no larger threshold, no larger questions, and no inherited deep pondering by poets, philosophers, and saints of these very questions. All is suddenly as plain as pikestaff. But it is not.

For a Christian, God is the Author of Life and Life is good. But we find ourselves in a world in which contingency, suffering, and malevolence are all too visible and seem written into the nature of things. How can these two acknowledgements be reconciled? Maybe, given our human limitations, they cannot be altogether but then neither can be rejected. Obviously, the age-long problem of evil in the world is too vast for our scope here. In such a world we must proceed with wide-open eyes but also with humility. We can and should hope for an eternity in which there is no suffering, where Love, Knowledge, and blissful peace coincide, the promise of which the Christian faith holds out to us, but we are not in it yet. These wider horizons seem faint in our experience but not in our recognition. They precede and determine the world in which we find ourselves alive as beings with Logos who must try to live in Love and accept that we will often enough fall away from Love and true Knowledge as will all those around us. Central to this faith is the Cross of Christ with the injunction that we should pick it up ourselves. Nothing could be further from the modern mantra that value only consists in the avoidance of suffering and discomfort. Nothing could be further from the Cross than the self-claimed 'dignity' of an assisted death.

There are areas in which we can be clear and other areas in which we cannot or, at best, only 'see as through a glass darkly' (1 Cor. 13:12). We always need to know where we can and should be clear and where we cannot. Those in favour of euthanasia, apparently, do have the advantage of clarity since nothing could be simpler than the reduction of thinking about what human life and death are and the place of suffering within it to two all too simple principles — first, individual choice and, second, suffering must always be ended by whatever means. The thinness of these principles, if widely accepted, which must have wide consequences beyond the instance of euthanasia, would turn us into the new conformists of a regime without a name but just as destructive of the properly human as Nazism and Communism. We live within the limits of our day-to-day experience, but we always have questions and intimations which frame that experience. We acknowledge something larger since, manifestly, we have not brought ourselves about and neither has the world in which we live. Death is a step into that unknown largeness about which we cannot speak or have certainty other than the questing certainty of faith. If the proponents of euthanasia are right, then there is no mystery in death at all and no encompassing largeness of human experience. We should always be in the safety, comfort, zone which blots out anything which threatens familiarly comforting and pleasurable horizons. And then we should call this progress. Their bluff should be called.

CHAPTER FOUR

Personal Experiences – Real-Life Stories

If the general arguments set out in the first part of this book and the fundamental Christian principles enunciated by St John Paul II are insufficient to persuade us to resist the propaganda in guises of mercy and care, then it might help if I share some of the experiences in my pastoral ministry that have fuelled my passion and support for Assisted Living rather than legally administering death.

Speaking out for End-of-Life Care

A parishioner once told me how her experience of patients 'agony as they were abandoned as death-bound set her on a journey to fight on their behalf in London. In her own words:

'Concern for the implementation of the execution of the advanced directive (ADR) onto the Mental Capacity Act 2005 caused me to travel to Parliament and voice my concerns to Sir Graham Brady the then M.P for my local area. I explained that from a purely observation Post I noticed that on Doctor's Ward Rounds when arriving at the bed of a patient whose treatment had been exhausted, the Team just passed the bed without consultation. Sometimes such patients were transferred to side rooms with little attention or none. With this real worry, I cautioned the above-mentioned ADR with the realistic concern that one could write one in a time of loneliness or rejection. Foresight of the possible consequence of the mental element cannot be proved either then or later. Foresight of the consequences of the facts and having regard to the way the case has been presented, in my opinion, an ongoing explanation is necessary to avoid misunderstanding. In these circumstances, it is dangerous and wrong to permit such provision of an A D R. Following that discussion with Sir Graham, various pathways have coincidentally been introduced into end-of-life care in hospitals and care facilities.'

Life and Family Saved by Faith

As a priest, I receive all sorts of calls and cries for help but when it is to notify me of an impending suicide, I try to be calm and invite the person concerned to come over for a chat before executing the planned act. I think he wanted a blessing over the phone that would supposedly free him of the guilt of ending his own life. Thanks to that phone call he is still alive today and is happy to share his own story:

'The support I have received since Fr Martin came to our community [Name withheld] in Northwest England about thirteen years ago has helped me through bankruptcy and consequently losing my family (moving abroad) before the forced sale of our home ten years ago. He had prepared me for my reception into the Catholic Church and for the sacrament of Confirmation and supported me thoroughly through suicidal ideation following the above events. I was diagnosed with Bipolar as a 28yr old Cardiac Surgical trainee (which immediately terminated that chosen career). Manic depressives have significantly increased suicides and my Christian Faith, supported by Fr Martin and other Priests/Ministers saved me from that fate. I have always believed that faith in Our Lord Jesus and his healing is an essential addition to medical treatment and complementary to controlling illness and its healing. By God's grace, my family, who had left to find refuge abroad, returned to me within fourteen months and we have rebuilt our lives back since. My career continued, initially, after surgery, retraining in psychiatry for several years and now in General Practice for nearly thirty years.

I agree with Fr Martin's argument about the Sacredness of Life. In the Eugenics of Nazi Germany, I may well have died in a concentration camp because of my Manic-Depression like many other persecuted groups in addition to Jews. Regarding euthanasia, especially for Depression, I absolutely agree it should be outlawed. Our Medical Profession is divided. For a long time, I have believed that Art and the Humanities and the Church (notwithstanding the Historic Catholic persecution of Galileo) need to contain possibilities yielded by Scientific advances.'

With hindsight, I think it is the thought that taking

his life was improper that has saved his life today and reunited him with his family to build a thriving home. What signal would legalising euthanasia send in this regard?

'Have you got time for me?'

In one of the parishes I have served (here in the Northwest of England), walking from the presbytery to the church one morning, a visibly disturbed young man approached me asking whether I was the priest and whether I had time for him. Finding it difficult to convince him that I was ready to listen to him, I promised to cancel all that day's appointments just to avail him of as much of my time as he wanted. This brought him to tears as he pulled a sharp knife from his pocket and dropped it at my feet. According to him, he was out to take his own life but did not want to die alone. He had decided to kill as many as he could before taking his own life, since according to him, this was such a wicked world filled with selfish people. No one cared and no one had time for anyone else. Drinks and drugs had not helped either as they only landed him in jail a few times. I listened to his story and offered what words of encouragement I could. About two hours later, he had moved from a depressing sadness, through unimaginable anger, and eventually to peace and joy.

It dawned on me how thin the borderline is between the will to die and finding joy in living, where love, care, and proper support are provided.

Always yield to God's Will - Mum's Experience – and 'I would choose to do it again!'

Watching my mother battle cancer brought home to me the mental and emotional anguish that could occasion the thought of euthanasia. It was an indescribably draining experience both for her and all around her. But, thanks to her faith and the support from family and friends, at no point did she think life was not worth it. She, amidst all the pain, led us in the family rosary prayer until she could no longer manage it. When asked to sign the 'Do Not Resuscitate' form, neither she nor any member of the family gave it a thought. She was looking forward to returning home from the hospital in London to see her beloved husband, my dad, again and to hold her newly born grandchild. Life was worth living till the end. Her final admonition to me was to always acquiesce to God's Will in the knowledge and trust that he had perfect plans for us, even when shrouded in mystery.

Similarly, Mary, a former parishioner, shared her story of looking after her parents till life's natural end and the mutual benefits of doing so: 'I looked after my Mum for four years and she needed 24-hour care. I could not leave her even for five minutes. I employed carers to help me with her personal care and her needs, feeding, changing bed sheets etc. She called my name all night every night for about three and a half of those four years. On several occasions, I was asked: 'Why don't you put her in a home?' My response was always 'She has a home here! She just needs more support at home'. Towards the end, when she was very frail, during what turned out to be the last week, I was asked by our doctor 'Would you like me to give her something to help her on her way?' I refused. She died three days later. Despite how hard it was, I would choose to care for her again in the same way. My brother's children were able to be here without any restrictions. Family members came and stayed. It was truly a wonderful experience of personal growth and spiritual transformation for everyone, not just my Mum and me. We went to Lourdes twice. My cousin came with us to help. I would choose to do it again. I have been at the death of both my parents, surrounded by family. My Mum showed me how to care for her in the way she gave me an example as she cared for her own mother. At the deathbed of my father, she prayed and invited Joseph, my Dad to let go, to 'let Our Lady and St. Joseph take you to Our Lord'. The evening before she died, I too followed her example and showed her a photo of my Dad and said, 'Come on now Mum. Let go... Look, Dad's waiting for you. Let Our Lady and St. Joseph take you to Our Lord'. She let go the following morning, indicating to me that, somehow, they were all there present, as she said, pointing with her right hand, 'Look!' She was ready and was taken naturally and peacefully. Both those deaths were powerfully moving experiences and felt surrounded by angels, by love and blessings, and by the wind of the Holy Spirit.'

The point is that the right spiritual and social environment will always play a significant part in the psychosomatic state of patients and the elderly. Investing more in an integral Assisted Living culture would improve the character of end-of-life and lead to a better appreciation of what is erroneously perceived as 'life unworthy of life'.

Tears of Joy: 'The happiest day of my life!'

Posted to serve in a small village in West Africa as a young seminarian, I resolved to visit every single home, whether Catholic or non-Catholic or of no faith at all. Two incidents left enduring impressions on me.

One incident was visiting a blind cripple who thought he was better off dead than alive. His wife had left him and remarried, as the situation became unbearable for her. The twelve-year-old son took over as the breadwinner and caretaker. With a leaky roof, he had pushed their beds from one side of the single room to the other to avoid the leaks, until there was no safe spot left. There were now two buckets on his father's bed to keep it a bit dry.

Deeply moved by this, I arranged for youths of the parish to come with me for a whole day's work, fixing the roof, tidying the house, and gardening. The presence of so many happy, enthusiastic, youths brought life to this household as we rendered every help possible to make them comfortable. The sheer joy, as the man asked all his neighbours to come and witness this gesture, cannot easily be forgotten. He found a reason to want to live again and crawled around sharing his story. Thankfully, members of his church community took notice and, I believe, looked after him and his son from then. Some years later, I was surprised to see them, represented by their church council, at my priestly ordination - even though non-Catholics - sharing this story with the congregation. It strengthened my conviction in the vital role of Assisted Living.

What stood out the most for me, though, was noticing that one of the young girls was in tears all the way back from that house. Upon enquiring what the issue was, she astounded me with her response: 'This is the happiest day of my life'.

Mistaken for Angels

Another incident was an old lady, locked up in a room and abandoned to die. I would have missed her were it not for a little child who called out to inform me that there was someone in that room with a bolted door.

She was a sorry sight; dried up to the bones, with hardly any flesh left on her, and could not make a sound. I had to rush home for cleaning materials as the stench from that room was horrid, of faeces, urine, and filth. She needed to be fed first, though, before the clean-up. So, we had to carry her outside to feed her first with whatever liquid food she could manage to absorb.

As soon as she regained strength and realised what was happening to her, her question - 'Please, are you angels?' - with such a calm but astonished voice, has stayed with me, with the attendant emotions. What joy on her face when we left her, as she pleaded for someone to help her invite neighbours to see her angelic guests! Once again, life was worth living. The story spread around the village and others were awakened to the duty of care towards this woman.

A Sister's Heartbreak

In a very moving case, the effects of which I personally observed, the sister of a patient was left in unending agony and fits after witnessing life snuffed from her sister at the authorisation of a niece who was the patient's next of kin due to proximity. The patient's face had lit up on seeing her sister (whom she had missed for years) and she clearly wanted time with her, but the next of kin had already signed for life's termination and wanted this quick enough to allow her to catch a flight to join her boyfriend for their pre-booked holiday. No plea from the sister could alter the process, as she had no legal standing in the matter. As her parish priest, I was left with the onus of assuaging this lady's pains on her return to England from the United States. It becomes apparent how people change their minds or act in certain ways when under great pressure, which would alter if the pressure were removed.

The Law as a Safeguard

Another parishioner has shared with me how the law became her last resort in the distress and overwhelming pressure from members of the family to accede to the ending of her sister's life. Here is her account:

'In the recent past, my very, very dear older sister was diagnosed with Motor Neuron Disease. The first effect of this horrifying diagnosis was the complete loss of her voice. Our only form of communication was via an iPad which she found onerous. I tried as much as possible to hide my extreme devastation from her which, thankfully, allowed for a little humour from time to time - "What did you do to deserve this"? I would tease. Her lovely smiling response gave license for some happy times together even in such difficult circumstances. Following home support supplied by another sister and me, she was able to manage for some time, but her rapid deterioration caused admission to a hospital and eventually Nursing Home. It was during the latter that, despite excellent care and everyday visits from both of us, she began to make strong inferences about the possibility of me helping her to end her life. Oh, how I examined myself; 'Are my visits and others, the excellent care, and the Faith we had been reared in insufficient to continue to stay with us?' It was to me that she made the direct question, although I had already been subject to indirect utterances from members of the family in favour of her opinion. I was acutely aware that the latter was coming from a place of sadness and suffering, especially from her two sons living some distance and possibly unable to watch their Mum suffering. However, I had to be strong and defend the truth in love. Our faith taught us that life is sacred from conception to death. We all had practiced that faith although some of us had stopped. How was I to communicate the right direction sensitively to my sister and the rest of the family amid divided opinions and mounting confusion that only aggravated the incredible pain and strain? I began with the law on criminal liability for complicity in another's suicide: 'A person who aids, abets, councils or procures the suicide of another, or an attempt by another to commit suicide, shall be liable on conviction on indictment to imprisonment for a term not exceeding fourteen years.' (Suicide Act

1961) s2). However, I very quickly alerted us to the fact that some States in the USA that retained the death penalty were researching the contents of the drugs used, as there was concern recently regarding the time and distress taken to die. I cautioned any attempt to discuss the subject of euthanasia with my very ill sister, pointing out that we could cause her further and possibly worse suffering. This explanation was sufficient and accepted by all and mercifully my sister passed away fairly peacefully shortly afterwards. I will be diligently following the discussion and voicing my objection to any changes in the law in this regard. (See Alabama case)'

This story corroborates another dissension at the UK parliamentary debate arguing that: 'As well as the pressure on the healthcare system to take this route, I worry even more about the pressure on patients themselves to request assisted dying if it is an option. It will be an option for almost everybody approaching death—that is the proposal. Clinical guidelines for many terminal or chronic illnesses will likely require doctors, at an early stage of planning treatment, to ask patients whether they would wish to have assistance in taking their own life. What a question to ask. Whatever the guidelines, every family will be required to have the conversation, in whispers or openly. In some families, we know how that conversation could all too likely go.'[57]

Assisted Living or Assisted Dying?

Clearly, Euthanasia is a very sensitive subject. I have tried to set out as clearly as I can the explicit arguments and less explicit assumptions that are used in its favour and which will be invoked to justify enabling legislation. And I have tried to set out with equal clarity what is wrong with these arguments and the severely restricted view of human life upon which they depend, and which will be inculcated, perhaps even enforced, if euthanasia is made legal. To these objections I have added some personal accounts of experiences directly known or reported to me. Sentiment and harrowing incidents should not be allowed to rule the roost in discussions about euthanasia, but it is obviously not simply a matter of rational and logical discourse. There is deep feeling and much knowledge of actual human predicaments in the arguments against euthanasia; it is not a prerogative of those in favour.

But we do need clearly thought-out arguments that can be widely understood. Catholics, for instance, will be (and indeed are already) faced with demands for reasons why euthanasia is unacceptable and will be accused of being 'dogmatic' and 'uncaring' in accordance with familiar stereotypes. It is important that they are prepared for this and can understand and present arguments which are to the point, intelligible, human, and undo these stereotypes and the often-vociferous propaganda. As I have tried to show, these arguments exist and have quite evident force. We should know them and use them.

St. John Paul, who was a very articulate and intelligent thinker concerned always with the essential character of human life, points us to the lessons from Africa which I earlier referenced, and with which I will conclude this book: 'The peoples of Africa respect the life which is conceived and born. They rejoice in this life. They reject the idea that it can be destroyed, even when the so-called 'progressive civilizations' would like to lead them in this direction. And practices hostile to life are imposed on them by means of economic systems which serve the selfishness of the rich". Africans show their respect for human life until its natural end and keep elderly parents and relatives within the family.'[58] Maybe it is this love, respect, and care for the elderly and the vulnerable that will provide the answer to the call for euthanasia. Hence, I absolutely agree with Cardinal Vincent Nichols, the Archbishop of Canterbury, and the Chief Rabbi, in their joint letter to Parliament, that 'the aim of a compassionate society should be assisted living rather than an acceptance of assisted suicide'.

APPENDIX

John Paul II's Teaching

The heroic latter life until death of St. John Paul who bore in the manner of a saint, but also that of an exemplary human being (the two are not opposed), suffering and pain till life's natural end, is permanently relevant here and must not be forgotten. It is the lived equivalent to his clear and courageous teaching .

Prominent in his Pontificate was this struggle between the "culture of life" and the "culture of death" which so marked the wars and dictatorship societies through which he lived For St John Paul, this is the external sign of the eclipse of the sense of God and of man and thus the systematic violation of the moral law".[59] His unswerving stand is that euthanasia is "a serious violation of the law of God, since it is the deliberate and morally unacceptable killing of a human person".[60] And so, no law or human authority can justify it.[61] Even in confusing cases he rightly argues that "the moral principle is well known, according to which even the simple doubt of being in the presence of a living person already imposes the obligation of full respect and of abstaining from any act that aims at anticipating the person's death." [62]

He insisted that "Human life is sacred because, from

its beginning, it involves 'the creative action of God', and it remains forever in a special relationship with the Creator, who is its sole end". Therefore, "God alone is the Lord of life from its beginning until its end: no one can, in any circumstance, claim for himself the right to destroy directly an innocent human being" (Gen 9:6).[63] This is decreed by God himself: "For your own lifeblood, too, I will demand an accounting and from man in regard to his fellow man I will demand an accounting for human life" (Gen 9:5).[64] Life, especially human life, is a gift that ought to be protected[65], and is always a good, since he is made superior to all other animals and so has a sublime dignity, based on the intimate bond which unites him to his Creator. Thus, St Irenaeus says "Man, living man, is the glory of God". For there shines forth in him a reflection of God himself.[66] This sacred element to human life grounds its inviolability, written from the beginning in man's heart, in his conscience.[67] In effect, the absolute inviolability of innocent human life is a moral truth,[68] which is discernible even by the light of reason[69].

John Paul II's principles are clear and rooted in Christian tradition but he is not just speaking to and on behalf of Catholics, for the tenets of the Christian faith, though not based on reason, are capable of rational defence and demonstration. That we are not in absolute control of life and death (and attempts to so be are both futile and destructive) is not solely a Catholic truth but a human one.

St. John Paul's teaching is manifestly in continuity with those of the great Fathers and theologians of the Church, especially with St. Thomas' condemnation of the taking of one's life or that of the other[70], and with Saint Augustine's teaching that "it is never licit to kill another: even if he should wish it, indeed if he request it because, hanging between life and death, he begs for help in freeing the soul struggling against the bonds of the body and longing to be released; nor is it licit even when a sick person is no longer able to live".[71] He unequivocally attests to representing the Church's teaching authority on this matter, as he declares: 'in harmony with the Magisterium of my Predecessors and in communion with the Bishops of the Catholic Church, I confirm that euthanasia is a grave violation of the law of God, since it is the deliberate and morally unacceptable killing of a human person. This doctrine is based upon the natural law and upon the written word of God, is transmitted by the Church's Tradition and taught by the ordinary and universal Magisterium.'[72] With regard to things, but even more with regard to life, man is not the absolute master and final judge, but rather he is the "minister of God's plan".[73] Though this does not preclude the legitimacy of an active sacrifice of one's life (martyrdom), if this stands in the service of God, in which case it will only be a noble act of giving one's life to the original giver. But the gift remains in God's hands rather than the will of the donor.

Suffering, here, intrinsic to all human lives (a fact of

experience and the burden of the expulsion from Eden story in the book of Genesis) is not something that can be used to deny the gift quality of human life or as sufficient reason for refusing the gift whenever we want to. Life is a given in which we find and found ourselves not something that we have ourselves selected on our own chosen terms. It is all too easy to let the shallow ethics of consumerism infiltrate our attitudes here.

Hence, with papal approval, on May 5, 1980, the Sacred Congregation for the Doctrine of the Faith, in its Declaration on Euthanasia, clarified thus: 'By euthanasia is understood an action or an omission which of itself or by intention causes death, in order that all suffering may in this way be eliminated. Euthanasia's terms of reference, therefore, are to be found in the intention of the will and in the methods used. It is necessary to state firmly once more that nothing and no one can in any way permit the killing of an innocent human being, whether a fetus or an embryo, an infant or an adult, an old person, or one suffering from an incurable disease, or a person who is dying. Furthermore, no one is permitted to ask for this act of killing, either for himself or herself or for another person entrusted to his or her care, nor can he or she consent to it, either explicitly or implicitly, nor can any authority legitimately recommend or permit such an action. For it is a question of the violation of the divine law, an offense against the dignity of the human person, a crime against life, and an attack on humanity. It may happen that, by reason of prolonged and barely tolerable pain, for deeply personal or other reasons, people may be led to believe that they can legitimately ask for death or obtain it for others. Although in these cases the guilt of the individual may be reduced or completely absent, nevertheless the error of judgment into which the conscience falls, perhaps in good faith, does not change the nature of this act of killing, which will always be in itself something to be rejected. The pleas of gravely ill people who sometimes ask for death are not to be understood as implying a true desire for euthanasia; in fact, it is almost always a case of an anguished plea for help and love. What a sick person needs, besides medical care, is love, the human and supernatural warmth with which the sick person can and ought to be surrounded by all those close to him or her, parents and children, doctors and nurses.'[74]

Addressing the participants in the International Congress on "Life-sustaining Treatments and Vegetative State: Scientific Advances and Ethical Dilemmas", John Paul states: 'With deep esteem and sincere hope, the Church encourages the efforts of men and women of science who, sometimes at great sacrifice, daily dedicate their task of study and research to the improvement of the diagnostic, therapeutic, prognostic and rehabilitative possibilities confronting those patients who rely completely on those who care for and assist them. The person in a vegetative state, in fact, shows no evident sign of self-awareness or of awareness of the environment, and seems unable to interact with others or to react to specific stimuli. Scientists and researchers realize that one must, first of all, arrive at a correct diagnosis, which usually requires prolonged and careful observation in specialized centres, given also the high number of diagnostic errors reported in the literature. Moreover, not a few of these persons, with appropriate treatment and with specific rehabilitation programmes, have been able to emerge from a vegetative state. On the contrary, many others unfortunately remain prisoners of their condition even for long stretches of time and without needing technological support. In particular, the term permanent vegetative state has been coined to indicate the condition of those patients whose "vegetative state" continues for over a year. Actually, there is no different diagnosis that corresponds to such a definition, but only a conventional prognostic judgment, relative to the fact that the recovery of patients, statistically speaking, is ever more difficult as the condition of vegetative state is prolonged in time.

However, we must neither forget nor underestimate that there are well-documented cases of at least partial recovery even after many years; we can thus state that medical science, up until now, is still unable to predict with certainty who among patients in this condition will recover and who will not. Faced with patients in similar clinical conditions, there are some who cast doubt on the persistence of the "human quality" itself, almost as if the adjective "vegetative" (whose use is now solidly established), which symbolically describes a clinical state, could or should be instead applied to the sick as such, actually demeaning their value and personal dignity. In this sense, it must be noted that this term, even when confined to the clinical context, is certainly not the most felicitous when applied to human beings. In opposition to such trends of thought, I feel the duty to reaffirm strongly that the intrinsic value and personal dignity of every human being do not change, no matter what the concrete circumstances of his or her life. A man, even if seriously ill or disabled in the exercise of his highest functions, is and always will be a man, and he will never become a "vegetable" or an "animal". Even our brothers and sisters who find themselves in the clinical condition of a "vegetative state" retain their human dignity in all its fullness. The loving gaze of God the Father continues to fall upon them, acknowledging them as his sons and daughters, especially in need of help. Medical doctors and health-care personnel, society and the Church have moral duties toward these persons from which they cannot exempt themselves without lessening the demands both of professional ethics and human and Christian solidarity. The sick person in a vegetative state, awaiting recovery or a natural end, still has the right to basic health care (nutrition, hydration, cleanliness, warmth, etc.), and to the prevention of complications related to his confinement to bed. He also has the right to appropriate rehabilitative care and to be monitored for clinical signs of eventual recovery.'[75]

In a homily during his Apostolic journey to America in 1999, John Paul passionately asked: 'As believers, how can we fail to see that abortion, euthanasia and assisted suicide are a terrible rejection of God's gift of life and love? And as believers, how can we fail to feel the duty to surround the sick and those in distress with the warmth of our affection and the support that will help them always to embrace life?'[76]

He is even more categorical with regard to laws in favour of euthanasia: 'Consequently, laws which legitimize the direct killing of innocent human beings through abortion or euthanasia are in complete opposition to the inviolable right to life proper to every individual; they thus deny the equality of everyone before the law. It might be objected that such is not the case in euthanasia, when it is requested with full awareness by the person involved. But any State which made such a request legitimate and authorized it to be carried out would be legalizing a case of suicide-murder, contrary to the fundamental principles of absolute respect for life and of the protection of every innocent life. In this way the State contributes to lessening respect for life and opens the door to ways of acting which are destructive of trust in relations between people. Laws which authorize and promote abortion and euthanasia are therefore radically opposed not only to the good of the individual but also to the common good; as such they are completely lacking in authentic juridical validity. Disregard for the right to life, precisely because it leads to the killing of the person whom society exists to serve, is what most directly conflicts with the possibility of achieving the common good. Consequently, a civil law authorizing abortion or euthanasia ceases by that very fact to be a true, morally binding civil law. Abortion and euthanasia are thus crimes which no human law can claim to legitimize. There is no obligation in conscience to obey such laws; instead there is a grave and clear obligation to oppose them by conscientious objection. From the very beginnings of the Church, the apostolic preaching reminded Christians of their duty to obey legitimately constituted public authorities (cf. Rom 13:1-7; 1 Pet 2:13-14), but at the same time it firmly warned that "we must obey God rather than men" (Acts 5:29) .... In the case of an intrinsically unjust law, such as a law permitting abortion or euthanasia, it is therefore never licit to obey it, or to "take part in a propaganda campaign in favour of such a law, or vote for it".'[77]

[1] Cf. Facing History and Ourselves, Holocaust and Human Behavior, Chapter 3, https://www.facinghistory.org/holocaust-and-human-behavior/chapter-8/unworthy-live, [Accessed 26 October 2021].

[2] Robert N. Proctor, "Culling the German Volk," in How Was It Possible? A Holocaust Reader, ed. Peter Hayes (Lincoln: University of Nebraska Press, 2015), 261.

[3] Cf. Robert N. Proctor, "Culling the German Volk," in How Was It Possible?, 261.

[4] Robert J. Lifton, The Nazi Doctors: Medical Killing and the Psychology of Genocide (23 July 2005), https://phdn.org/archives/holocaust-history.org/lifton/LiftonT021.shtml [Accessed 26 October 2021].

[5] A saying attributed to George Santayana, which in its original form read, "Those who cannot remember the past are condemned to repeat it."

[6] St. John Paul's teaching was so extensive and clear that I have gathered together some important material from his writings and summarise his teaching (and its acceptance in magisterial documents) in an appendix.

[7] https://www.wma.net/policies-post/declaration-on-euthanasia-and-physician-assisted-suicide/. Accessed 09/05/2023.

[8] https://www.usccb.org/committees/pro-life-activities/life-matters-doctor-assisted-death. Accessed 09/05/2023.

[9] https://www.usccb.org/committees/pro-life-activities/life-matters-

doctor-assisted-death. Accessed 09/05/2023.

[10] William E. May, Catholic Bioethics and the Gift of Human Life, (Huntington: Our Sunday Visitor Inc., 2000), 238.

[11] Sacred Congregation for the Doctrine of the Faith, Declaration on Euthanasia, Vatican, May 5, 1980.

[12] N.M. deS.C. art. in New Dictionary of Christian Ethics and Pastoral Theology, ed. David J. Atkinson, et al. (Illinois: InterVarsity Press, 1995), 358.

[13] Timothy E. Quill, "Death and Dignity" in Last Rights: Assisted Suicide and Euthanasia, quoted in William E. May Op Cit., 239.

[14] William, E. May, Op. Cit., 241.

[15] Fletcher, "The Patient's Right to Die", Quoted in William E. May, Loc. Cit.

[16] Nigel Bigger, Aiming to Kill; The Ethics of Suicide and Euthanasia, (London: Darton, Longman and Todd Ltd. 2004), 24.

[17] N.M. deS.C. Op. Cit., 358.

[18] Elochukwu, E. Uzukwu, A Listening Church: Autonomy and Communion in African Churches, (Oregon: Wipf and Stock Publishers, 2006) (1st Published by Orbis Books 1996), 25.

[19] Karl H. Peschke, Christian Ethics, Moral Theology in the Light of Vatican II, (Bangalore: St. Paul's Press Training School, 1992), 310.

[20] Bernard Häiring, Free and Faithful in Christ, Moral Theology for Priests and Laity, Vol. 3 Light to the World, Salt for the Earth, (London: St Paul's Publications, 1981), 86.

[21] Ibid., 314.

[22] https://www.usccb.org/committees/pro-life-activities/life-matters-doctor-assisted-death. Accessed 09/05/2023.

[23] N.M. deS.C. Loc. Cit.

[24] Loc. Cit.

[25] https://hansard.parliament.uk/commons/2022-07-04/debates/65B4AB0B-D148-42C6-8D8B-43AAC29219FB/AssistedDying. Accessed 22/05/2023.

[26] Veritatis Splendor, 38-45; 65;71)

[27] Address of John Paul II to the Participants in the International Congress of Life Sustaining and Vegetative State: Scientific Advances and

Ethical Dilemmas, 20th March 2004; See also Evangelium Vitae, 20.

28 Gaudium et Spes, 27.

29 Germain Grisez, The Way of the Lord Jesus; Difficult Moral Questions, Vol.3, (Quincy Illinois: Franciscan Press, 1997), 211.

30 Nigel Bigger, Op. Cit., 32-33.

31 Op. Cit., 35-36.

32 William E. May, Op. Cit., 161.

33 Bernard Häiring, Op. Cit., 86.

34 Nigel Bigger, Op. Cit., 115.

35 https://hansard.parliament.uk/commons/2022-07-04/debates/65B4AB0B-D148-42C6-8D8B-43AAC29219FB/AssistedDying. Accessed 22/05/2023.

36 Veritatis Splendor, 12, 13; John Paul II Address to the Participants in the 19th International Conference of the Pontifical Council for Health Pastoral care, Friday, 12 Nov. 2004.

37 Evangelium Vitae, 66.

38 John Paul II Address to the Participants in the 19th International Conference of the Pontifical Council for Health Pastoral Care, Friday, 12 Nov. 2004, 2.

39 Karl H. Peschke, Op. Cit., 310.

40 Peter Singer (ed), A Companion to Ethics, (Bodmin Cornwall: MPG Books Ltd, 1991), 296-297.

41 Thomas Pazhampallil, S.D.B., Pastoral Guide, Vol.1, Fundamental Moral Theology and Virtues, (Bangalore: Kristu Jyoti Publications, 1995), 1278. See also Karl H. Peschke, Loc. Cit.

42 Catechism of the Catholic Church, 2278.

43 Evangelium Vitae, 25.

44 CCC. 2277.

45 Pope Pius XII The Prolongation of Life: An Address to an International Congress of Anaesthesiologists. November 24, 1957.

46 Kevin, O'Rourke, O.P., "Evolution of Church Teaching on the Prolongation of Life," Health Progress (January-February 1988), 28-35.

47 Sacred Congregation for the Doctrine of the Faith, Declaration on Euthanasia, Vatican, May 5, 1980.

48 William E. May, Op. Cit., 261.

[49] John R. Connery, S. J., in William E. May, Op. Cit., 258.

[50] J. Daniel Mindling, John Paul II: Dying with Dignity, https://www.usccb.org/prolife/john-paul-ii-dying-dignity. Accessed 22/05/2023; John Paul II, "The Inalienable Rights of the Disabled" Address to the Pontifical Council for Pastoral Assistance to Health Care Workers, November 21, 1993; John Paul II, Address of to the Participants in the International Congress on Life-Sustaining Treatments and the Vegetative State: Scientific Advances and Ethical Dilemmas, March 20, 2004.

[51] Pius xii, "Religious and Moral aspects of Pain Prevention in Medical Practice", Address to the Ninth National Congress of the Italian Society of the Science of Anesthetics, (February 24, 1957), http://www.sspx.org.

[52] Evangelium Vitae, 65.

[53] Ladaria Ferrer, Humanae Vitae as a bold and prophetic encyclical: Its relevance today, https://newdailycompass.com/en/humanae-vitae-bold-prophetic-and-increasingly-relevant; https://www.congreshumanaevitae.org/en/return-on-the-humanae-vitae-congress/. Accessed 23/05/2023; Cf. Congregation for the Doctrine of the Faith, Samaritanus Bonus, on the care of persons in critical and terminal phases, 22 September 2020.

[53] Ladaria Ferrer, Op Cit.

[55] The International Theological Commission, Communion and Stewardship: Human Persons Created in the Image of God, https://www.vatican.va/roman_curia/congregations/cfaith/cti_document s/rc_con_cfaith_doc_20040723_communion-stewardship_en.html#:~:text=According%20to%20Gaudium%20et%20Spes,man%20the%20name%20of%20God. Accessed 22/05/2023.

[56] Gaudium et Spes, 76.

[57] https://hansard.parliament.uk/commons/2022-07-04/debates/65B4AB0B-D148-42C6-8D8B-43AAC29219FB/AssistedDying. Accessed 22/05/2023.

[58] John Paul II, Ecclesia in Africa, Post-Synodal Apostolic Exhortation, of The Holy to the Bishops Priests and Deacons Men and Women Religious and all the Lay Faithful on the Church in Africa and its Evangelizing Mission Towards the Year 2000, 43.

[59] Evangelium Vitae, 21.

[60] Evangelium Vitae, 65.

[61] Evangelium Vitae, 74; John Paul II, International Conference on the

Elderly, by the Pontifical Council for Pastoral Assistance to Health-Care Workers", Saturday, 31 October.

[62] John Paul II, Address to the Participants in the International Congress on "Life-Sustaining Treatments and Vegetative State: Scientific Advances", Saturday, 20 March 2004.

[63] Evangelium Vitae, 53; Donum Vitae 5.

[64] Evangelium Vitae, 39.

[59] John Paul II, International Conference on the Elderly sponsored by the Pontifical Council for Pastoral Assistance to Health-Care Workers, 31 October.

[66] Adversus Haereses, IV, 20, 7: SCh 100/2, 648-649, Evangelium Vitae, 23, 34.

[67] Evangelium Vitae, 40.

[68] Evangelium Vitae, 57.

[69] Evangelium Vitae, 2, 77, 82.

[70] ST. 11, 11, q 64, a 5.

[71] Evangelium Vitae, 66.

[72] Evangelium Vitae, 65.

[73] Evangelium Vitae, 40, 52.

[74] Sacred Congregation for the Doctrine of the Faith, Declaration on Euthanasia, Vatican, May 5, 1980.

[75] Address of John Paul II to the Participants in the International Congress on "Life-Sustaining Treatments and Vegetative State: Scientific Advances and Ethical Dilemmas", Saturday, 20 March 2004, 2-4.

[76] https://www.vatican.va/content/john-paul-ii/en/homilies/1999/documents/hf_jp-ii_hom_19990127_stlouis.html. Accessed 22-06-2023.

[77] Evangelium Vitae, 72-73.

Author of:

Mary - Daughter Zion: An Introduction to the Mariology of Joseph Ratzinger (Benedict XVI), 2021,
By
Peter Lang Ltd, International Academic Publishers, Oxford, United Kingdom.
And
Actio Divina: The Marian Mystery of the Church in the Theology of Joseph Ratzinger (Benedict XVI), 2021,
By
Peter Lang Ltd, International Academic Publishers, Oxford, United Kingdom.

Printed in Great Britain
by Amazon

24137461R00079